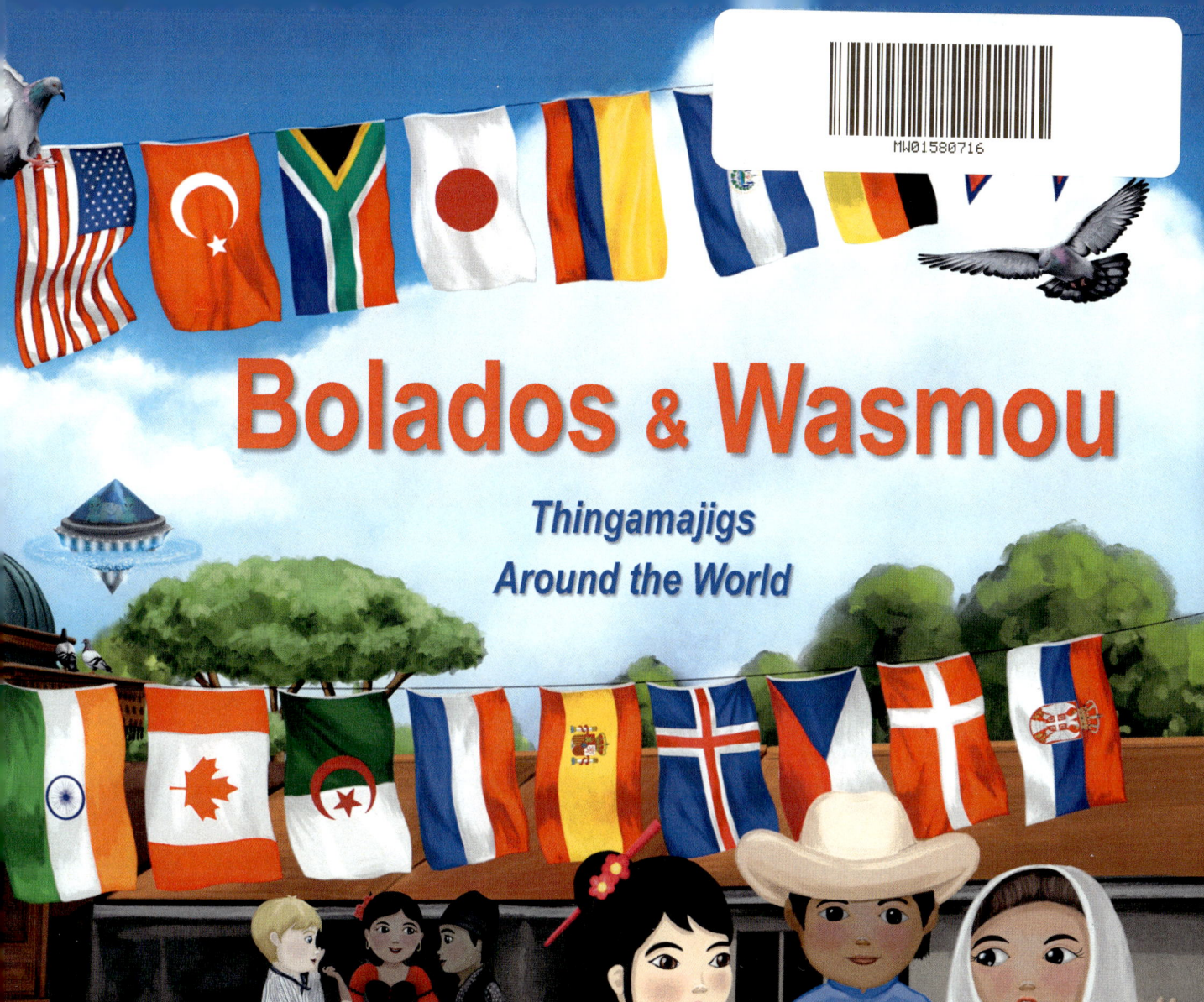

Bolados & Wasmou

Thingamajigs Around the World

KEITH SYLER

Illustrated by
JULIE SNEEDEN

Everyone remembers...
...and we also forget
the name for that thingy,
but don't get upset.

Extra words are
special ones, too,
to help you define
that bing-a-ma-boo.

It's not so often,
without any prediction,
you see something,
and words defy your description!

When this thing flew by last night,
it gave the neighbors a terrible fright.
They told the 9-1-1 operator, "It's awfully big...
this... this... thingamajig!"

Madi was brave
and probably breathed, *"Whooh,"*
after the police showed up
to meet her and her *wasmou*.

Oh yes, that's how in Arabic
we name a thing-a-ma-boo.
It flew off too soon,
but what about me and you?

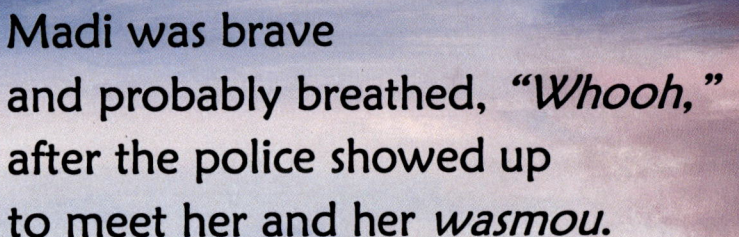

I'm Mohktar from Algeria,
and I go fast too.
My carpet is turbocharged
and brand-spanking new.

Fasten your seatbelt,
load up for this gig,
and let's see if we can catch
that thingamajig!

Mohktar flies high on his rug
but me, Engin, I ride low.

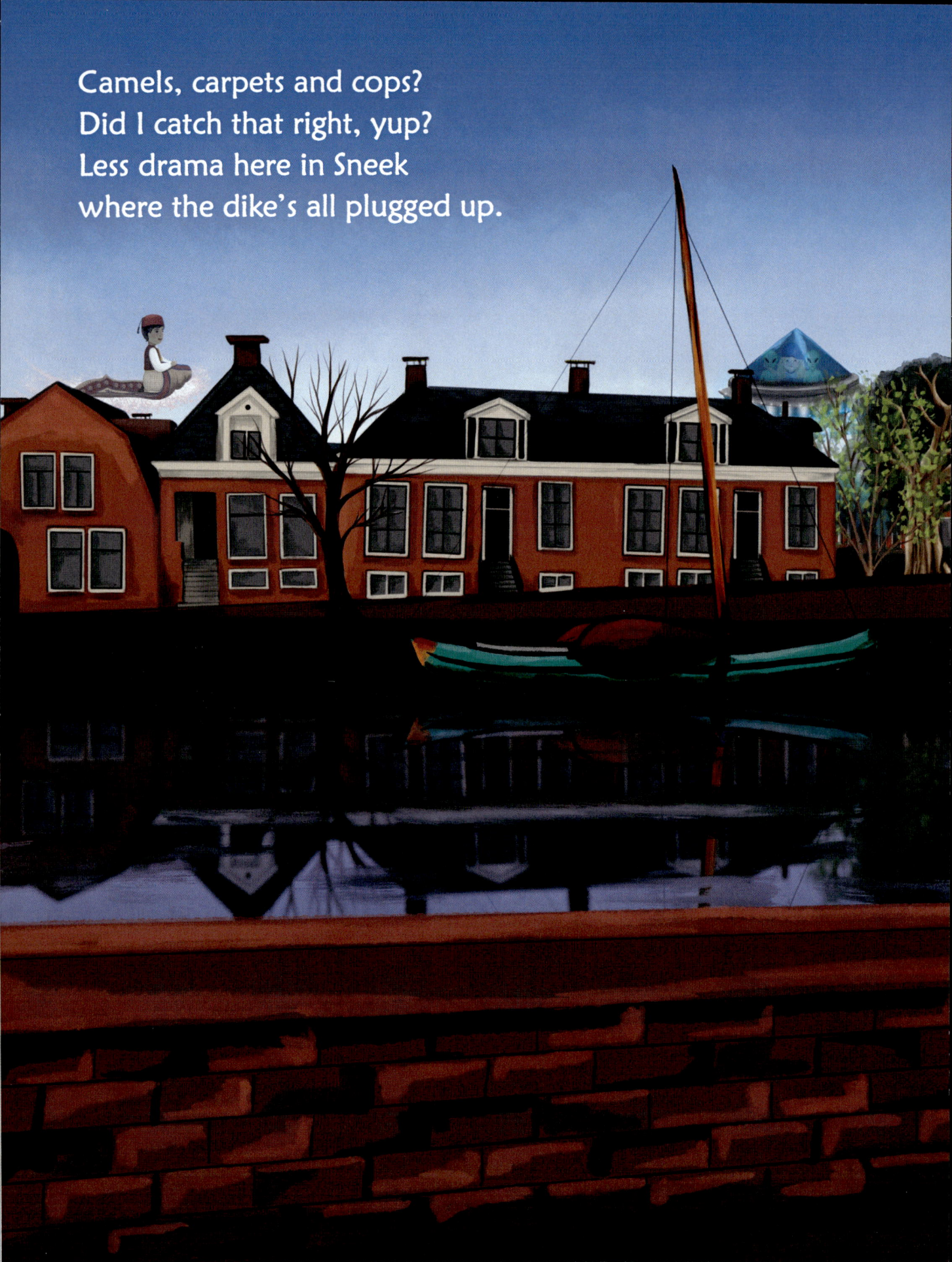

Camels, carpets and cops?
Did I catch that right, yup?
Less drama here in Sneek
where the dike's all plugged up.

I saw all this talk and thought, "FEE FI FO FUM,
I smell the blood of an Englishman!"

I'm Blunderbore, the Giant, and angry I am.
Listen close, whether daughter or son.
When I lack the word in German,
it's a *Dingsbums*.

Oh Giant, don't be crabby.
We've got a word in Punjabi.
I'm Urvashi, and in India
some call it *habbijabbi!*

(Actually it's Bengali, but don't tell my daddy!) Look! It's a bird, no... a plane... No, it's Madi!

I'm Honsa and my mom
thinks it's a load of bunk,
but while looking for thingamajigs
I found a slam-dunk.

In Czech we call the thing
a *tentononc*.

I'm Andrea from Spain.
You ask what's the ruckus?
An important subject
has fallen upon us!

I'm Binod, from Nepal.
Some things I simply know,
like loyalty, forgiveness, and patience...
and you reap what you sow.

But back to our subject before I take off and go.
We've got thingamajigs too.
They are *falano*.

Hi, Binod! My name's Robinson,
I'm from Isla Barú.
That's a spot in Colombia
with an ocean view.

Come visit for coffee
and dance the Macarena.
When we don't know the word,
we call it a *vaina*.

I'm Anja, from Denmark.
You know I'm so cute...
We've got that word, too.
We call it a *dut!*

Different words at first
sound like gobbledygook.
If you yell them out loud
all will think you're a kook.

I'm Marie-Jo in Québec.
Here's for the very astute.
We call our thingamajigs
machins, and also, *trucs*.

I'm Trevor in South Africa.
Thanks to Mandela, Tutu,
and others of us,
we have a constitution
that's totally righteous.

There's also a word in isiZulu for that thing-a-ma-jigga... Obviously, it's an *intazinga!*

Hola, I'm Marcelo,
a Salvadoreño.
Thingamajigs in other lands?
Those words I don't know!

But listen closely
then repeat it nice and slow.
In Salvadoran Spanish,
they are *bolados.*

This thingamajig matter deserves an inquiry.
We're Kristín and Már and golly oh gee,
here in Iceland with our volcanoes so fiery,
we sometimes soak in hot water
and think about *fyrirbæri*.

PRONOUNCE THE WORDS!

Use these phonetic pronunciations or an online tool and say it like a local.

Arabic:	**wasmou** WAH-smoo	Nepali:	**falano** fah-la-NO
Turkish:	**zamazingo** zah-MAY-zin-GOH	Spanish: (Colombian)	**vaina** BIE-nah
Dutch:	**huppeldepup** HOO-puhl-de-POOP	Danish:	**dut** DOOT
Japanese:	**nani nani** NAH-nee NAH-nee	Serbian:	**stvarčice** STVAHR-chee-say
German:	**Dingsbums** DINGZ-buhmz	French:	**machins / trucs** mah-SHAN / TROOK
Bengali:	**habbijabbi** HAH-bee-JAH-bee	isiZulu:	**intazinga** in-tah-ZING-ah
Czech:	**tentononc** TEN-to-NOHNK	Spanish: (Salvadoran)	**bolados** boh-LA-dos
Catalan:	**daixonses** die-SHON-sus	Icelandic:	**fyrirbæri** FEER-ee-BIER-ee

Copyright © 2024 Keith Syler
All Rights Reserved

ISBN: 978-1-64649-456-9 (paperback)
ISBN: 978-1-64649-460-6 (hardcover)

This humble book is dedicated to Marie Dlasková and her son Jan "Honsa" Dlask.
He was taken from us too soon,
while doing his work as a professor of languages,
in December 2023. *Ahoj*, dear Honsa.

About the Characters

Some of the characters in this book are named after real people from around the world.

Madi is a teacher with Baltimore County Schools.
Mohktar is a carpenter and contractor.
Engin is a tax-credit attorney.
Darren is a professor of political science.
Miwa is a nurse.
Urvashi is an attorney and animal rights enthusiast.
Andrea teaches Spanish in Barcelona.
Binod is an entrepreneur.
Robinson works in language and commerce.
Alida is an attorney.
Marie-Jo is a chiropractor and also works in pedagogy development.
Trevor is a beloved author, comedian, and media personality.
Marcelo is a student in the Baltimore City Schools.
Kristín is a professor of anthropology.
Már is an associate professor of finance.

...No aliens were harmed in the production of this book.

Also available by this author and artist:

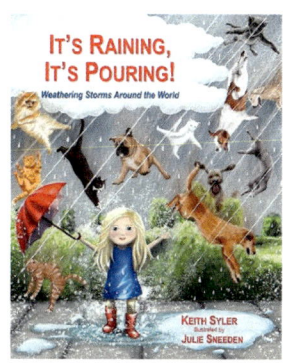

ABOUT THE AUTHOR

KEITH SYLER is a semi-retired lawyer, educator, and lifeguard. He presently resides in Baltimore, Maryland.

When a teenager, Keith worked for his township, near Fredericktown, Ohio. He operated a tractor with a large hydraulic lawnmower apparatus to cut grass and trim tree branches alongside the roads. Some exclaimed, "What's-his-face took that thingamajig and thunder-whacked our thoroughfare!"

Keith later encountered, as we all do, other thingamabobs, devices, and contraptions. His favorites are those that help people get clean drinking water, like pumps and filter systems.*

*check out livingwatersfortheworld.org. They are experts!

About the Illustrator

Constantly inspired by the words and tales of imaginative authors, **JULIE SNEEDEN** uses color, light and creativity to bring her artwork into these magical worlds. To make the character of her images come to life, she draws upon a palette of thingamajigs including watercolor, pencil, charcoal, digital illustration, photography, and oil paints.

Julie studied Fine Arts in KwaZulu Natal, South Africa, but now lives with her family in the UK. Reading stories to her children has inspired her over the years to pursue the art of illustration. She has illustrated numerous stories to amazing authors all over the world.

Made in the USA
Middletown, DE
30 October 2024

63410789R00024